15 Consejos:
A Guide for Latinx Students to Succeed in College

Published by Fundamental 21 Publishing Company
Printed in the United States
Designed by Miguel Rodriguez
Copyright © 2021 by Alvert Hernandez
ISBN: 978-1-7367623-2-5

Dedication

To all the Latinx students on their campuses trying to find their way,

To my two sisters, Arlin & Aisha, that push me to be the best brother and man that I can be,

To my amazing fiancée, Myra and soon to be wife who believed in my dream,

To all the amazing educators that believed in me and pushed me to earn not just one degree, but two.

This one is for you.

Tables of Contents

1. Understanding Institutional Types

2. Navigating the Financial Side of College

3. Leaving the Nest

4. Finding Your Tribe

5. Selecting A Major

6. Mentorship & Sponsorship

7. Pa'lante, Siempre, Pa'lante

8. Social Media Education

9. Student Organizations

10. Fraternity & Sorority Life

11. Disfrute el Colegio

12. Con Qué Tiempo?

13. Mental Health in the Latinx Community

14. We Are Not A Monolith

15. Consejos De Amigo

Introduction

The Latinx population is the fastest growing minority population in the country. According to the Postsecondary National Policy Institute, approximately only 20% of Latinx students will be enrolled in 4-year colleges and universities across the country. While colleges and universities continue to increase Latinx student enrollment, support for those students do not. Latinx students are often forced to fend for themselves to navigate the massive institution of higher education. The majority of Latinx students are also first generation—and if you add socioeconomic, race, and class to the mix, students will find themselves with additional barriers to overcome.

As a first generation Latino male, I had to learn everything about college on my own. I was extremely fortunate to meet tremendous individuals along my college career, who helped me realize my potential, while also helping me navigate higher education. I stand on the shoulders of their greatness and I owe them a debt of gratitude.

The inspiration of this book comes from meeting some of the coolest people I have ever met and being able to pass this knowledge onto others, in hopes that this book will help change the lives of others looking to pursue a college education.

This book will be written from my perspective, utilizing the years of experience I have earned throughout the time I have survived, lived, and worked in education. I aspire to offer a fresh perspective that is relatable to the new generation of college students.

I've always said that higher education is a game. And like any game, there are a set of rules, tricks, and strategies to win. From deciding what type of college/ university to choose from to deciding your career path, this book will discuss it all. I will be tying my own identity as a Latino male and cultural understanding of the Latinx community to these specific areas. This book will compile those in 15 different focus areas to promote awareness and Latinx students' success at any college or university.

1
<u>Understanding Institutional Type</u>

As a high school senior, I did not fathom the complexity of the college process. I had slightly below average grades in a public school district that did not prepare the majority of students for collegiate success. I was a first generation Latino male and the first in my family to go to college—and only because it was forced on me. In this chapter, we will discuss the different types of institutions and their designations. I will be covering as many as I can by adding my own personal and professional experience.

It is extremely important that you visit these institutions first and decide on your school afterwards. The college selection process is such a personal decision and there is no "right" way to do this.

If you are applying to college now, this section can help you make the most educated choice on what college is the best fit/ has the best resources for your intended career path.

Two-year Community College

For a start, I'm going to talk about community colleges because they are wildly underrated. Community colleges have amazing faculty and staff that prepare students for the next chapter of their lives.

Majority of your first two years at the college level will be filled with prerequisite[1] classes anyways, and you might as well attend a community college to complete them.

They are SIGNIFICANTLY cheaper and with the same quality of education. You could be paying, on a national average, $5,000 a year for community college vs. $30,000 a year for a 4-year public institution. That is a massive difference in pricing for students that struggle with getting financial assistance and are forced to pay tuition out of pocket. Some states also offer partnerships with community colleges to significantly reduce the cost of attendance. Public and private 4-year institutions across the country are making it easier for folks to earn a bachelor's degree after completing community college.

Community colleges can also be a very popular decision for our students that will be commuting from home or have other financial responsibilities in their families.

La familia is a huge part of our students' lives and community college can offer the flexibility to complete a degree while managing our commitments at home.

---

[1] Prerequisite: Classes that are required to take before advancing in your major

Four-year public college/university

The four-year public colleges/ universities can offer a more "traditional" college experience to students. They have residence halls for students interested in the residential experience and often have several campus amenities, like food options, gyms, access to technology/ science labs, and a variety of study spaces. Oftentimes, college campuses can be a microcosm of the real world and almost a "world within a world" feel.

There are different types of 4-year public schools. There are predominately *residential* vs. *commuter* based institutions. You can determine this by seeing the number of students that live on campus versus the number that commute. Depending on your circumstance, I would recommend you choose a school that fits your situation. Larger commuter student schools have unique resources and tools to enhance the commuter experience. In the same token, large residential campuses have amenities that make the living on campus experience worthwhile.

Private Institutions

The private school sector is a beast. Often, Latinx students from low-income households shy away from applying to private schools because of the large sticker price.

If you are looking at colleges/ universities, please do not let the sticker price deter you from applying. Most private schools offer incredible discount rates for students and some lucrative packages to entice you to stay.

Private schools understand that they need to be competitive to recruit a diverse group of students, therefore, I strongly encourage you to negotiate with private institutions for more financial aid and scholarship awards. Are you bilingual? Are you biracial? Do you come from a multi-generational home? These are all unique factors that private institutions are looking for.

If you were a high achieving, high school student (regardless of high school district), you can utilize your class ranking, extracurriculars, and diverse background to your advantage to secure the bag. Do not settle!

Private schools will offer a more individualized experience and will sell you on the "you are more than a number" philosophy. If small class-room sizes, close contact with faculty, and relationship building with staff/ peers sounds good to you, consider looking at private schools.

Some private schools are religiously affiliated. This will probably show up in the campus culture, events/programs they offer, and in the classroom. Before applying, look at how the affiliation may or may not affect your experience as a student and consider this very closely before committing.

Liberal Arts & STEM/Technical institutions

Colleges and universities can also be broken down by specialties. Liberal arts institutions are schools that challenge their students to be critical thinkers. Their curriculums often pick and choose from different areas; from the sciences, history, literature, mathematics, philosophy, and many others to ensure their students are well-balanced after graduation.

Technical or STEM[2] based institutions are hyper focused and often academically rigorous institutions because of their area. There is a ton of research that indicates STEM institutions have the highest return of investment for a college student because of the high paying jobs and push for STEM education in the United States. As a Latinx student, if STEM excites you, this could be one of the best institution types for you to enroll in.

---

[2] STEM: Science, Technology, Engineer, Math

HSIs vs. PWIs [3]

I have discussed different types of institutions and now I want to discuss the different designations institutions might have because of student enrollment. If you are a person that cares a lot about WHO you are going to school with, this section will be very important for you to pay attention to. There are more student designations, but I will focus on these three for this chapter.

HSIs are schools that have at least 15% of students with Hispanic descent enrolled at their institutions. \

HSIs are given federal—and sometimes state—grants for programming and administrative support, to help develop and ensure the success of Hispanic students.

HSIs will have programs in Spanish and might have more faculty/ staff of Hispanic/ Latinx descent. However, it is very important to know that just because you attend a HSI does not mean you will be at a predominately Hispanic based institution. HSI designation is only 15% of the enrollment number, meaning, if the school has 10,000 students, only 1,500 students have self-selected that they have some form of Hispanic descent.

---

[3] HSI: Hispanic Serving Institution
PWI: Predominately White Institution

PWIs are—unfortunately—the most common type of institution. It is important to note that all colleges/ universities will have their issues with systemic racism, oppression, elitism, and classism. These issues are pervasive across all institutions and institution types. HSIs are not immune to these issues. I make this point because Latinx students need to know that the college/ university you are in may and will continue to perpetuate these 'isms. Please know that you are not alone and I hope you find at least one thing in this book to thrive as you pursue your degree. Before choosing an institution, you should ask yourself—what matters to me? Is it flexibility? Is it the amenities the school offers? Is it a specific major or career path? All these and more are important questions to answer before committing yourself to an institution. If you are already enrolled—that is okay! Now that you have this background knowledge on institutions, you can work to tailor your experience and get the most out of your college experience. I hope that the remaining chapters in this book resonate with you deeply.

2
<u>Navigating the Financial Side of College</u>

For most people, the most challenging part of going to college is managing the financial burden. Pursuing your degree is one of the biggest investments that you can make. Therefore, it is important to ensure people know what they are signing up for. Not knowing how to navigate the process can mean you miss deadlines or lose out on a ton of money.

If you are reading this and still in high school, PLEASE take your high school GPA seriously. You will be shocked at how much money you can earn to go to school if you maintain a top GPA. Slacking in high school can literally cost you THOUSANDS of dollars in the long run.

Huge disclaimer—I am not a financial aid expert or financial guru. I am going to speak from my years of experience in working in higher education and also my own personal experience from my student days. You will notice I will constantly recommend you to your financial aid advisor throughout the chapter. This chapter will discuss some helpful pieces of advice and additional information to consider while navigating college.

Before enrolling, make sure to complete your Free Application for Federal Student Aid commonly known as FAFSA. As implied in the name, you do not need to pay to complete this application. I know there are a ton of services out there that will charge you and try to scam you into paying—please do not fall for those.

Completing your FAFSA and connecting your application to the institution you apply to will help you secure federal funding. The amount of money you receive is contingent on a ton of factors, primarily from your parents or legal guardian's income.

I strongly recommend that everyone connects with their Financial Aid office at your respective institution upon enrollment and maintain that relationship throughout your undergraduate career. There are so many changes that can happen to your financial aid package and having a trusted financial aid advisor at your institution is a huge must.

Shop Around for the Best Deal

Consider applying to multiple institutions even if you do not have an intention of attending that school at first. Treat yourself like a high commodity (mostly because you are!) As Latinx students across the country are attending institutions more than ever before, they are woefully underrepresented at private four-year institutions.

Higher Education is as much a business as anything else, and some institutions (including private ones) will be willing to offer you more money than others. This is where your high school transcripts, involvement, and other extracurriculars can really set you apart from the rest of the pack. Most institutions across the country are trying to recruit a "diverse" student body (and if you are reading this, you are most likely Latinx, so check that off as diverse) If money is a big motivator for you to attend institutions, consider casting a wide net during your application process.

Understanding the Financial Aid Package

You never want to play with your money. So, one thing you want to double and triple check is the financial aid package from your institution. In this chapter, we will break down different types of funding that an institution will offer you and define some terms. However, the main thing you need to know is how much money an institution is giving you vs. the cost of attendance. By doing that, you will know how much money you need to pay out of pocket or take out in loans.

Understanding the financial aid package is also important because institutions offer so many different types of funding. Beware of institutions offering partial scholarships. These may look attractive for a year or two, but then you have to figure out how to cover the difference in the future. Ask direct questions to your financial aid advisor. Make sure you know exactly what you are getting yourself into, before fully committing to the institution.

Grants vs. Loans

Grants are usually funds that a student does not have to pay back. They can be federal, state, institutional, or even private grants that are dispersed to students. Very few grants have stipulations that are put on the student, but it is important to verify that with your financial aid office just to be sure.

Loans are funds that are allocated to a student with the expectation that the loans will be paid back. There are federal loans from the government and private loans. Federal loans have lower interest rates and some federal loans do not charge you interest while you are still enrolled and up to 6 months after you leave or finish your degree. The first time you ask for a federal loan, you will be asked to complete a Master Promissory Note. A Master Promissory Note is essentially a contract explaining your responsibility in paying back the loan. The form will go over very basic information about how interest will accrue on your loan.

Personally, I recommend sticking to the federal loans only if they are absolutely necessary for you to pay off your balance. Depending on your financial situation, you might have to take additional private loans and explore other options. Since I am not a financial expert, it is difficult for me to comment on the private loan options. However, I would advise you consult your financial aid advisor and do extensive research if you choose to explore private loan options.

Scholarships

Scholarships are awarded to students depending on a variety of different factors. There are different classifications of scholarships available to students. You can find scholarships through the institution you are applying to, but also beyond. There are websites and so many organizations that offer scholarships to students, the key is finding those opportunities. The different types of scholarships include (but not limited to) need based, merit based, athletic, micro, and even employer scholarships. In this section, we will break each of these scholarship types down. Need based scholarships are given to a student that demonstrates extreme financial need. Your financial aid office will be able to determine if you would qualify for any of these need based scholarships. Some of these scholarships can also have a GPA component tied to them as well, so if you are still in high school, KEEP UP THOSE GRADES.

Merit based scholarships are given to a student that has high academic achievements. A merit based scholarship can be awarded because of your class rank, high school GPA, AP/ Honors classes, and other academic related achievements. Institutions set their own scholarships and also set their own criteria for awarding merit based scholarships. You might earn yourself a merit based scholarship at one institution, but find yourself not earning one at another institution you applied. This is another reason why I strongly recommend applying to as many institutions as you can because you never know what institutions will offer you!

Athletic scholarships are pretty cut and dry—they are given to students that play a sport. Something to note is, not all institutions can offer you an athletic scholarship. Division III schools are not eligible to offer scholarships to their student athletes for their sport, but will offer a variety of merit-based aid and other institutional aid. Sometimes, that can equal to a full-ride, but sometimes it does not.

Micro scholarships are smaller scholarships often in the hundreds of dollars and only offered one time to the student. This is different from an institutional need based scholarship that often lasts for the duration of the student's time at the institution. Micro scholarships can help pay for books, parking, and other supplies you will need.

Employer scholarships are offered by selected employers to their employees. These scholarships range in offering but can help student employees significantly reduce the cost of tuition as long as they remain working at their part-time job and remain in good standing. Some examples of employers that offer a tuition assistance program or scholarships are McDonalds and Starbucks. If you have a part-time job off campus, consider asking if your employer offers tuition assistance or reimbursement. Do not leave any potential money on the table. Any amount can make a huge difference!

On Campus Vs. Off Campus College Jobs

Working part-time or even full-time during your college career is not unfeasible, especially if you have a strong need to make ends meet—having a job might be a requirement rather than a luxury. There are pros and cons with having an off campus job vs. an on campus job and I will talk about some of the tangible benefits you can get from either or. One is not better than the other and depending on your situation, you might not have a ton of options.

Let's begin with on campus jobs. On campus jobs have a variety of benefits, but the number one benefit is flexibility. Being a student worker on campus allows you to prioritize school first and then work second.

Your supervisor will understand when you have exam periods and might even flex your schedule in advance without having to ask. You will be able to make some money on the side without having to work a significant amount of hours.

Some on campus jobs allow you to even do some of your homework assignments while working. Depending on the type of job you have, your down periods can be filled with doing reading assignments or submitting that paper for your next class.

Your on campus job will usually be a maximum of 20 hours per week, which gives you plenty of time to either pick up another job or focus on your school work. Student worker positions also help you develop connections with other administrators on your campus that can help with relationship building. These types of jobs are usually developmental and teach you professional etiquette.

Some student worker positions offer some unique benefits that all students should consider. For example, if you are living on campus, you can apply to be a Resident Assistant and be a student worker within the residence halls. Usually, institutions will cover a portion of your room and board (or cover it completely!) or pay you a stipend. Some other student worker positions can offer you the ability to register for classes early, free parking on campus, or tuition discounts.

Finding an on campus job can sometimes be a difficult process for students. Some departments will post their social media pages while others will post a flyer on campus. The key is to connect with people you know have the connections. Speak with student leaders across campus and administrators you have connected with to see what positions are open. You might even find that they can recommend you directly for the position or walk you through the application process.

Off campus jobs can be a mixed bag and very difficult to predict how well they will accommodate your school schedule. In a future chapter, we will talk about strategies on how to navigate your off campus responsibilities, but for now, off campus jobs offer an insight on the working world. You might not get the days off; you need to study for your exam or have the flexibility of studying while at work. You will have to manage your time extremely well to account for the time travelling to your job, school, (and home for our commuters).

Your off campus job might offer you more hours and a better pay, which is something that can be applying to some folks. If your college is far away, you might be able to ask for a transfer so you work closer to your institution. While working to pay for school, some off campus jobs will also help you if they offer a tuition reimbursement or tuition assistance program. It might be worth the time to check with your employer to see if they have such a program or find a new job in the area that offers that type of program.

Having an off campus job can give you a much needed break from being on campus. If you live on campus, work on campus, and do not have a car, you can easily feel trapped and stuck at your institution. Having an off campus job can give you that much needed break where you find yourself doing something completely different for several hours a week. This job can be an opportunity to get your mind off of all the papers and academic stress and a much needed break from your physical environment.

Your off campus job can also be an extracurricular opportunity that can give you more experience in the field you wish to go into. You can be utilizing the classes and theories in the classroom and applying them in the field while you are at work. Trust me, this will strengthen your ability to relate to the material and even encourage you to engage in the classroom. You can utilize your experience in your papers, research, and even find ways to double dip between your classes and your job. You might even be able to impress your supervisor with some of the technical knowledge you are learning in the classroom!

Overall, it is so hard to recommend having an on campus vs. an off campus job. It depends so much on your personal financial situation and your own needs. No need to absolutely push yourself if you do not have to. If you have time to balance both, you should certainly think about finding opportunities that compliment your area of study and bolster your resume. Unless the job you currently have is the career you like, remember that the job you have now is mostly temporary. You have bigger goals and aspirations than where you are right now. Do not lose sight of where you want to be because you are focusing too much on where you are right now.

Semester Workload

A great hack to save money at most institutions is understanding the amount of credits you can take without having to pay additional fees. At most institutions, your tuition costs for a full-time student will remain the same for a certain range of credits per semester. For example, most institutions require you to take 12 credits to remain as a full-time student. The costs of your tuition will be the same whether you take 12 credits that semester or even 18 to 19 credits.

Some semesters, you might take a lot more rigorous classes and some might be easier on you. Being able to plan ahead will be able to save you a ton of headaches in the future. Attempt to take a higher class load in a semester when you know you have less work responsibilities, or are able to focus more heavily on your classes. You might want to dial back when you need to re-shift your priorities.

Managing your semester to semester workload is a great hack to save yourself thousands of dollars attending four year institutions and potentially finishing a half year to a year early. This is only recommended to students that are very strong academically and can handle a high amount of classes at the same time. The goal should be to take at least 15 credits a semester if you aspire to complete your 4-year degree on time.

Satisfactory Academic Progress

I wanted to include this in this chapter to warn you that your grades are directly linked to your financial aid. If you are receiving any sort of federal aid from the government, failing your classes will result in you losing your funding. Your funding is tied to your Satisfactory Academic Progress and failing more than half of your classes for one semester will result in you being placed on probation.

Some institutions will flood you with resources and some institutions will challenge you to seek those resources out yourself. Failing more than half of your classes for two consecutive semesters will result in you losing your financial aid awards.

Also, being under a certain GPA can also affect your ability to receive federal funding. You will then be asked to come out of pocket for the difference, which could potentially mean you are out of school because the cost of attendance is just too high.

This is a huge difference from high school to college and many students may understand what failing does to their grades, but sometimes do not understand what it does to their pockets. Staying on top of your academic progress is extremely important to ensuring your success, because if you cannot pass your classes or pay for your school, it will be pretty hard for you to succeed.

Well, sometimes you go through things in life and class might not exactly be your number 1 priority at the time. Totally understandable. If you are facing extenuating circumstances, please make sure to connect with your academic advisor immediately. There are many things you can do ahead of time that can help you make sure you do not lose that funding.

One example is taking the withdraw option. Taking a withdrawal (or taking a W as known on most campuses) is a process that allows you to remove yourself from a class without penalty. If this class is a requirement for you to graduate, you will be asked to take that class again in the future. If it is not a requirement, you can elect to take another class in the future that satisfies your requirement.

Now, each institution has their own policies around this, but you usually can do this without penalty for up to a certain point in the semester. Most institutions allow you to do it up until the midterm part or half part of the academic semester. The W will show up on your transcript, which future employers can see, but it will not affect your GPA. I strongly recommend you utilize Ws sparingly throughout your college career and do not take one every semester.

Refund Checks

Refund checks is a hot topic for students all around the country. You might receive a refund check because your financial aid package outweighs the cost to attend the institution. Your refund might come because of a scholarship or because of a loan. Remember earlier in the chapter we discussed the difference between a loan and a grant. If you are taking out loans and receive a refund check, that is still money you have to pay back in the future.

If you do not need to take out loans, try to avoid it to the best of your ability. It is very tempting to take out that 4k loan and have it deposited into your checking account to spend throughout the semester, but do you really need it?

Your school loans should be utilized for educational expenses only, but sometimes, students elect to ball out. Ask yourself, is this loan that will come in a form of a refund check absolutely necessary or not? Personally, I had to take out a couple of loans while going to college (especially in my graduate program) to cover my cost of living and bills. Utilize the excess loan as a possible last resort if need be while at your institution and exhaust all other options first.

If your refund check is because of a scholarship or other grants that you received, you are in luck! This is money that you do not have to pay back and can utilize it as you see fit while you are in school. You may need to purchase food, school supplies, parking, etc. with these funds, so be frugal and make sure it lasts. Your refund check should be your little nest egg while you focus on your academics. This might mean you cut back on Uber Eats and eat in the cafe a little bit more or take that train instead of that Uber. I have had 10k in my account and 10 dollars in my account, and I can promise you my 10 dollars have always lasted longer.

Hidden Fees

There are a ton of fees to take into account from your institution that is not automatically loaded onto your bill. One of the biggest fees that you will spend money on is books. Books can be astronomically expensive. I found myself always playing the barter game every semester, trying to find the cheapest possible book options for my classes. In this section, I am going to put you on some tricks/ tips to save yourself coins while attending school.

Books will run you a ton of money if you are not careful. I have spent over $100 on ONE book in a semester alone, so try to find cheaper alternatives before purchasing them. An option is to ask if the book is in the campus library. Ask your professor if there is a loaner copy available and either make copies of the book or take pictures on your phone. I literally did this every semester and uploaded the pictures to my Google drive. I took notes electronically, and deleted the pictures on my phone to save storage (especially since I only had like 16 GBs while I was in undergrad!)
Another option is to consider going half with a friend in the class. This will cut the cost of your books in half and you can share the books whenever you need. Students are always reselling their books back on their social media pages and posting it on campus Facebook pages. If you want the book and you know you will be utilizing it frequently, think about buying it used off another student for significantly less than the new price.

You can also elect to buy an older edition of the book and utilize that in your class. For this option, I strongly recommend you speak with the professor first before you waste your money on an older edition that will serve you no purpose. The last option is to find the books online by checking out some of the most popular book websites right now. Never buy your book for your class before you speak with the professor. I have had so many professors in my career tell me that, "Oh, I don't really use the book" and you find yourself spending your hard earned money on the book for no reason. Do not feel shy about asking your professor what their expectations are for book usage.

Parking is another huge expense if you commute or plan to have a car on campus. Some institutions will charge you per semester or per academic year. My last institution, I was an employee and still had to pay $500 for parking, per semester. PER SEMESTER! That is $1,000 gone right off the top. It is important to weigh your need for having a car on campus and find a parking plan that makes the most sense for you, but be prepared to pay for parking at your institution every semester.

Some majors will charge you additional fees. Depending on the major, you might get charged with lab fees for science majors or extra supplies you will need for a class.

For example, my math class required me to buy a code that was more expensive than the book to do the assignments. Although the book was cheap, that code was over $100 at the time and something I did not plan for during my first semester in college. These additional fees should be listed in the syllabi for the class or you can ask your advisor for any knowledge they have on those classes before you register for them. Some additional fees that are not included in your tuition costs include your graduation fee that some institutions charge you (yes, some schools will charge you to graduate, I know it is crazy) and will be required for you to pay your last semester.

The last hidden fee that isn't so hidden is your school supplies. You are going to need notebooks, pens, pencils, and most certainly some kind of electronic device. A high end laptop can cost you in the four figure range and is certainly not cheap if you do not have one before entering college. Although it might not seem like a lot, these fees add up throughout the years you spend studying, so make sure you stock up and have a good amount of supplies before the semester begins.

3
Leaving the Nest

Being a college student regardless of whether you commute or live on campus requires you to metaphorically "leave the nest" and become more independent. In the process of doing this, you might feel the guilt of leaving your family members "behind" or guilty as a result of your focus being elsewhere, instead of helping out at home. I know I did. It can sometimes feel like the two worlds are pushing you apart from each other. In this section, we will explore how to begin the process of leaving the nest.

Managing Expectations

If you are a first generation college student like myself, odds are that your family has no clue what you are going through. There are a lot of things that they do not understand because of the drastic change from high school to college. One of the first things to do is to manage your parents/ guardian/ family's expectations as you embrace your new journey. Share with your family your new schedule. I remember having to explain to my family that night classes exist and I was not spending all my time "*en la calle*".

For Commuters still living at home: The space in which you do your school work is extremely important. Think about your posture and the location of where you are doing your learning/ study/ work. Believe me, it is extremely difficult to participate in a remote lecture while *Primer Impacto* is playing in the background. Try to find different times during the day that are quieter around the house or develop a makeshift "home office" in your own room or living room area.

Plan for additional time spent on campus so you can take advantage of on campus events. Your institution will offer a variety of programming available and we will discuss this further in later chapters. However, start by attending at least one or two events a month in your first semester. Incorporating it into your schedule will help you with the transition to college by forcing you to spend some more time at your institution and becoming more acclimated to college life.

For Residential students living on campus: Start off by developing a relationship with your college roommate (most likely you will have one) and try to get to know them. Most colleges/ universities offer some form of "roommate agreement" that can be filled out to serve as a contract on how you plan to live together. Also, connect with your RA [4] and learn more about the opportunities they have to offer and the expectations for living on campus.

Become aware of your surroundings. It is important to note if you are living in a completely new area, learn what is around your college. If you now live very far from home, you might need to find a new barber (for my fellas, I know it might as well be the end of the world), find where you are going to get your nails/ hair done, find some new food spots, etc. Take the first few days scouting the land and do not be afraid of asking some upper-class students these questions. I mean, how else can you be successful if you are not looking fly?

---

[4] RA: Stands for Resident Advisor. This is an upper-class student that works and lives on your hall that serves as a mentor and helps build community on the floor.

Develop a routine for your classes, studying, work (if you have a job), socializing, and taking care of your personal needs. When you were home, perhaps some of these things were taken care of *(maybe you always had some good food waiting for you in the kitchen, or your laundry was done)*, but now it is your responsibility to be independent. Do not forget to schedule time to call home or be prepared to receive random calls from the *abuelos* or mom/ dad randomly checking in. This idea of you living away from them will be new for them as well, and developing a routine to check-in and maybe even visit home during the semester is important to set strong expectations.

In this chapter, we spoke about some much needed tips and suggested topics to focus on addressing before leaving the nest. Below, there is a chart split into two areas and you can add your checklist items here. You can take some of the ideas that were mentioned in this chapter or decide to add your own ideas below. The goal should be to add a total of 5 to 10 checklist items of your own and hold yourself accountable throughout the process!

Commuter Checklist

Residential Checklist

4
Finding Your Tribe

When you look at the big picture, college can be a daunting thing to look at. You see all the requirements you need to complete over a course of four years, all the money that you have to pay, and the expectation of graduating with a career in hand …Where do you even begin? How do you even know who has your best interest? Some people look like your biggest fans, but secretly giving you the *mal de ojo*[5] from the sidelines. It is awfully difficult to get to the finish line without developing that real "tribe" of people that will help you get through it. In this section, I will dive into the different ways to find a collective of folks that will enhance your educational experience.

Not All Skin Folk Are Kin-Folk

I begin with saying this—not all skin folk are kin-folk. I remember hearing that somewhere several years ago and it struck me. Sure, I have been wronged by white people before, but none grimier [6]than by folks that look like me—share similar pain and upbringing as me. It's devastating, appalling, and certainly not expected. As we discuss being vulnerable and opening up to others in this chapter, I want you to always proceed with caution.

---

[5] Mal de ojo: Translates to Evil Eye. Latinx culture believes that receiving this can mess up your good fortune.
[6] Grimy: An action that is deplorable. Basically anything that is fucked up.

Latinx people are not a monolith[7]. Just because someone may look like you, speak the same language as you, or even has the same nationality as you, does not mean that they will back you all the time or care about your best interest. In college, it is important to forge relationships with folks that will protect, guide, and respect you for who you are. Always.

Begin in Your Classes

Look around in your classroom. Peep how people move from day to day and see who operates in similar ways as you. Take advantage of what you can learn from some of those cheesy icebreakers your professors force you to do in the beginning of the semester. When it's time to pick other people for group projects, try to pick others you know have similar interests as you or even your same major.

Find ways to formulate a "working" group or a study group. I think my entire junior and senior year of college was me finding at least 3 people in each class that I can trust. We would compare notes, ideas, and even strategies to survive the class. This helped build some much needed trust and got us through some tough times—especially with some of these crazy professors nowadays.

---

[7] Monolith: A group of people that are perceived to be the same.

Professors

Your tribe does not have to be just your peers. I am going to admit—I am an old soul. So, when I got to campus, I immediately gravitated to some professors. You will know who the real ones are on your campus real soon. Most of the upperclassmen know who they are and some might even refer you to their office hours.

Professors can be invaluable members to your tribe. They often have a lot of institutional knowledge and know who the movers/ shakers are on the campus. I recommend that you make time and attend a professor's office hours regularly. Office hours are open times that professors schedule for students to drop in, ask questions about class, and build genuine relationships. This is an absolute major key if the professor is in your major and you know you will take another class with them.

Professors have a ton of connections with their field and are required to do research for the institution they work for. Do some digging online regarding what your professor's research focus was and see if that matches your interest. Those are the professors you should actively be building a relationship with. They can help you secure an internship or get you connected with more people in the field you want to be in.

Administrators/ Staff

I am going to try and remain as unbiased as possible here, but administrators/ staff on campus are slept on. Each institution has a ton of administrators, but a few key players. From my own experience, some of the best people I know that changed my life are college administrators. These folks work at institutions because they want to help students every single day. Find the folks that are real early in your academic journey. Every institution is different, but I want to shout out a couple of different departments/ areas you should check for some dope people that can help you in college. This list is not all encompassing and only has some of the greatest hits.

- Residence Life department
- Student Life/ Leadership office
- Commuter Affairs/ Office
- Diversity/ Inclusion/ Equity/ Multicultural Office
- Women's Centers
- Latinx Centers (If you are BLESSED to have this on your campus)
- Financial Aid Office
- Academic Advising Centers

Student Leaders

We are going to talk about student clubs and organizations in a later chapter, but I want to acknowledge some of the real movers and shakers at institutions across the country. I would strongly recommend you connect with the student leaders on your campus because they are often students with a lot of drive, passion, and resources. You want people with those traits to ride with you.

You can find student leaders at major institutional events and even on the institution's website. Take some time during your busy schedule to check out student led events that they are hosting. Student leaders will be the most honest with you and can give you the inside scoop of all things to know regarding the institution. They can help you connect with great professors, administrators, and even give you some suggestions on the best food spots around.

Dime Con Quién Andas, Y Te Diré Quien Eres

This is something my mother and abuela would say almost every day. As a young boy, this is something I rarely paid mind to and now this is something I think about every day. Who is part of my day to day circle? How are they helping me advance and better myself?

I learned this early in my college days when I saw that the people in my circle were not growing with me. No shade, but when you start to move on a different level, you need a different team. I found new people at my undergrad that grew with me and I even consider some of them family.

Pay attention to the people you are with at your institution. They will influence a lot of what you DO and what you DON'T do. You want to surround yourself with a tribe that challenges you to grow and try new things—that support your endeavors, pray for your success and support you when you fall. If you find yourself being a part of a weak circle, it might be time to ask yourself who you are.

Who are the top 5 people in your circle that you talk with every day? I want you to list them below and then elaborate a little bit on why they are in your circle. Are they adding or subtracting from your greatness?

1. _____
2. _____
3. _____
4. _____
5. _____

_____

_____

_____

_____

_____

_____

5
Selecting a Major

Selecting a major can be one of the most stressful decisions you can make as an undergraduate student. Even when you apply to an institution, they are already asking you what major you are intending to pursue without you stepping foot on the campus. A major is an area of study you focus on while you pursue your degree. A major often has a series of classes within a department while including additional experiences to fulfill degree completion. Students are coming into college with all different levels of understanding regarding selecting a major. In this chapter, we will discuss the many factors to consider when selecting a major.

So…What Do You Want to Be When You Grow Up?

Ah, the age old question. I am sure adults have been asking you this since as long as you can remember. Now, you are "grown up" and have major anxiety thinking about picking what you want to be for the rest of your life. I want to ease some of those nerves for you—the major you intend to study will not be what you do for the rest of your life.

Millennials[8] and now Generation Z[9] are changing jobs and careers at a much more frequent rate than previous generational groups. Your parents or grandparents might have worked one or two jobs their entire lives, but the research suggests that is completely different now.

When you are selecting a major, think about what type of career you would like. Some folks already have the answer to this, but some are still exploring (which is totally OK!). You can do some quick Google search and see what degrees/ majors those individuals have earned. Outside of the careers that require specific licenses or exams (i.e. teaching, law, medicine) I am sure you will see that the degree choices are incredibly diverse. All majors and degrees are not created equal, so think strategically on which major suits you best and not the other way around.

Major Does Not Define You

Your major selection will not define who you are for the rest of your life. As mentioned before, you may pursue a major and end up in a totally different career path after graduation.

---

[8] Millennials: According to the Pew Research Center, this age group is considered between 1981-1996
[9] Generation Z: According to the Pew Research Center, this age group is considered between 1997-2012

The major you select will open up doors for you in certain fields, but your work experience and further education will dictate future career options. Your major is not a personality trait—please expand your options when pursuing your degree. I was an English major. I thought I was going to utilize my degree by being an English teacher (lol, sike), but I have been on a completely different course!

Industry Stalk

If you know what type of career you would like after you complete your degree, go follow folks on LinkedIn and other social media platforms. Check out their talks and see what type of majors they pursued when they went to college.

You can learn a lot from listening to successful people and might even pick up a thing or two that will help you along the way. Their majors (amongst many other things) probably helped them achieve the skills they need to excel in the industry. There are so many students I know that claim they want to be a doctor, but do not know any doctors. How do you really know that is what you want without doing that research?

What Your Family Wants Vs. What You Want

This is a pretty big one for some folks. Some students feel indebted to their family to go into the "family business" or another high paying job without having the passion to do that work. I promise you there is money to be made in any field. However, you are not going to be successful and make money in a career you hate. When choosing your major, you need to ask yourself—is this because I want it or because my family wants this? Your family might be scared of you graduating with no job prospects, so they pressure you into pursuing a specific career because of high pay or connections in that area.

Sometimes, your family might not be well versed in higher education to properly advise you on what areas to study. They might not know what your degree is actually about or what you plan to do with your degree. I was definitely one of those students. I am not going to lie to you, when I graduated with my English degree, the first thing my mother said was, "So you got a degree in a language you spoke your whole life?" At first, I laughed so hard because I knew she was trying to be funny, but I knew she had no idea how challenging it was to earn that degree. Regardless of major, earning your degree is a life-changing achievement and at the end of the day, it is YOUR degree. Study what you want!

Importance of Skill Building

The emphasis on your major should not be more important than the emphasis of building skills. Look at your choice of major and see what type of skills you build from earning that degree. For example, my English degree helped me construct strong arguments in writing and in speaking. It helped strengthen my analytical and critical thinking skills. You want to choose a degree that will complement your future career path or build you transferable skills that you can apply in a wide range of career options.

The key is to speak with advisors, talk with current students, and look at the class descriptions that are offered in that major before making a selection. What trends are you noticing when you ask about your intended major? You want to know that the major you are selecting is helping you build transferable skills that can be career specific, but also transferable to other opportunities. Some key things to look for when picking a major that can help with skill building,

- *Internship opportunities that are built into the program for some firsthand experience.*
- *Research opportunities with full time professors*
- *Partnerships with nearby companies in your field of interest*

- *Adjunct [10]professors with work experience in your field of interest*
- *Professional development opportunities like conferences, speakers, and related student organizations*
- *Additional certifications earned while obtaining your degree*
- *4+1 programs that offer the opportunity to receive a master's degree more quickly*
- *Flexibility to obtain a minor[11]*

Take a Personality/ Career Assessment Test

I recommend this regardless of where you are in your major journey. Your life experiences will change how you view the world, which can affect how you score on personality and career assessment tests. Most institutions will offer some form of career aptitude test out of their career or advising offices. Take advantage of that resource as a student and schedule an opportunity to meet with someone in that office to go over results. You might encounter some careers you have heard of before, but also some other careers you might know never existed.

---

[10] Adjunct: Part-time professors that usually teach at multiple institutions or still work in their field.

[11] Minor: A smaller program you can complete while obtaining your degree. Typically, 6 to 7 classes are required to earn a minor.

This also can help you find a career that helps you align your strengths, passions, and values all in a career that can actually make you some money. Sometimes, people believe that they have to work for money and do what they love as a hobby and do not realize the unique ways to combine them. This can be your main source of income or an opportunity to find a 2nd income or side hustle.

What Lights Your Soul on Fire

Selecting a major is also about finding what you truly enjoy doing or "lights your soul on fire" is a term I truly enjoy. You can reflect on the first two semesters of classes and see what classes made you the most excited. It could be the professor, the assignments or even you genuinely interested in the material that can push you to selecting that major. You will do better in a major that you are excited about and the goal should be finding something that you are not consistently dreading for four years.

Balance your major with a minor that you absolutely love. For example, you might love theater as a hobby, but not something you would like to major in. Minoring in theater will help give you other transferable skills that will compliment your major, while at the same time fulfilling your passion for theater. That is just one example of the different possibilities you can explore to keep you engaging with your passion areas.

Aligning Your Values with Your Career

Another way to determine if the major and career choice is for you is to do some reflection on your values. Understanding what motivates you and what your values are can help you make a decision that is congruent with those. Folks will change careers for a variety of different reasons throughout their lives, and one of those reasons is because they do not feel that their work is valuable anymore. Check in on yourself regularly and making sure the work that you do (and aspire to do) is congruent with your values.

Assessing the Job Market

For my analytical folks, make sure you crunch the numbers on your future job market. Your field may be oversaturated right now, but numbers could drop by the time you complete your degree. Analyzing your field can help you fill in the gaps and address some of the most popular demands employers are looking for in the job market. If employers are looking for technological skills, make sure that you build a strong portfolio in your undergrad degree with technology certifications and other experiences.

The major you select should be preparing you with skills and knowledge on future job opportunities—some jobs that might not even exist yet! It is great to know the principles and the basics, but you also want a major that will prepare you for what is to come. You do not earn your degree and suddenly stop learning, you will need to continue your education in your field by staying up to date with current trends and best practices. A major should give you the skills to be able to excel in that field right now, but also in the future as well.

Maximizing Your Return On Investment on Your Major

Another analytical point to follow up on is the return on investment (ROI) on your degree. Return on investment means how much money you are profiting from your degree. It is very common for folks to look at the return of investment as a metric for deciding what degree to obtain.

As you pay your way through college or see your overall school loan balance increase, people want to know that their investment in their education is worth it. There are proven majors that give you the skill sets needed to secure a high paying job upon graduation.

As I mentioned before, only utilizing this metric without taking into consideration your skills, passions and values is a recipe for disaster. Proceed with caution.

Furthering Your Education

Do you know if you will be furthering your education after your bachelor's degree? If the answer is yes, selecting your major will help you significantly with your future educational goals. Your major should give you the skill set needed to give you the edge in graduate school. Any research, books you have read, and classes taken can help you tremendously in your graduate degree, if related. Keep all your papers, projects, and assignments stored on your drive because they will be invaluable to you as you climb the educational ladder.

Even as an undergrad, look at what future graduate programs are looking for from applicants. Some programs might require certain prerequisite courses, internship hours, GPA, or some combination of the three. Knowing your requirements can help you know what goals you should achieve before finishing your undergraduate degree.

6
Mentorship & Sponsorship

Mentorship is something not talked about ENOUGH in our own community. When I talk about mentorship, I am not talking about that really old person that gives you great advice. Sure, that is a part of mentorship, but mentorship is so much more robust than that. Mentorship is something white people have been doing for years. As a Latinx community, we need to talk about the importance of mentorship and about sponsorship. Mentorship is about relationship building. I will be sharing with you some "go-to" people, but ultimately if you do not vibe with them, it is time to find someone else. In this chapter, we are going to break down the construct of mentorship into different areas and define sponsorship in our community.

Mentorship Comes in Different Forms

The first part is redefining the way we view mentorship. When I first thought about a mentor, I envisioned some old person "taking me under their wing". I thought mentorship is one-sided and strictly helps the mentee secure a job. I also thought you could only have one mentor at a time.

Mentorship is multi-faceted, complex, and comes in different forms. Think about mentorship as focused as professorship is. Do you have ONE professor for Biology and English? No. In life, you need multiple mentors for different aspects in your life. Since mentorship is such a massive area, I will be breaking down the different forms of mentorship you should seek throughout your college career.

So...How Do You Ask Someone to Mentor You?

This is a question I have often received after speaking with a group of students. There is no "right" way to do this, but there are definitely a lot of ways to mess this up.

You want to start by identifying what the time commitment is going to be. Mentors are often mentoring multiple people at the same time and their time is extremely valuable. Think about connecting with this person over social media or scheduling a time to meet with them during their office hours *(if they are on your campus)* to discuss it further.

Are you able to meet on a weekly, bi-weekly or monthly basis? What would you like to gain out of this mentorship and how can you contribute/ help your mentor on any projects they might be running? Setting tangible expectations helps from the start can be a great way to break the ice.

At the end of the day, it is hard to completely eliminate the awkwardness of asking someone to mentor you. Lean into it and be yourself. As long as you are being yourself, you will be OK. Remember, real recognize real.

Academic Mentor

The Academic Mentor is someone that has a mastery over your major. This could be a very impressive senior student, professor in your major, tutor, etc. I strongly recommend a senior professor in your department as your first attempt. They can break down what classes are offered when, what classes can give you the necessary skills for advancement, and explore electives in your major that excite you.

This person can help shape your academic experience at your institution and help guide you through that journey. 120 credits is the standard to graduate at most institutions, which means you have a TON of coursework to shape/ mold to your needs. You can convert some hands-on experience on an internship to academic credit as well as a research project. Your academic mentor can guide you through this process.

Career Mentor

The Career Mentor is someone that understands your strengths and has connections in the field you wish to work in. This could really be any staff or faculty member at your institution. The career mentor can help you remove the blinders and limitations you have placed on yourself.

For me, I was limited in my understanding of possible career choices when I was in college. I came to the institution wanting to graduate and be a teacher. That is all I ever knew. My career mentor helped me understand that there are other ways to be in education without being a teacher. They helped normalize my transition from my career focus of being a teacher, to being an educator. This was invaluable to help get me on the right path.

This person will help you get connected with others in that field. You can learn about others' experiences in that field and even gain an internship/ job opportunity in the process. As you build your network, you can begin to think about specific areas that you wish to gain knowledge in. The more informed you are about your career while you are in college, the more you can utilize college to best set you up for employment in that field after you graduate.

Cultural Mentor

The Cultural Mentor is someone that "gets it" and understands where you come from. This person has strong cultural competencies and can make you feel at home although you are at college. They can get you connected with cultural programs, nearby food spots that remind you of home, or even can even sit in the office and speak your language.

Research has proven that seeing more people that look like you helps break down imposter syndrome and boost academic efficacy. These barriers are very real and as Latinx students, it is important to have a cultural mentor in your corner. If you cannot find a cultural mentor in your institution, think about connecting with established folks from different institutions via social media. Listen to podcasts and check out YouTube channels to find that cultural mentor—even if it is in a digital format.

Personal Mentor

The Personal Mentor is someone that you truly confide in. This person is someone you feel comfortable going to talk about your life. This mentor cares about your emotional well-being and has a personal interest in making sure you succeed in all your endeavors.

At times, this person might believe in you more than you believe in yourself. A personal mentor is someone you may instantly vibe with. This is probably someone you will have in your life far after your college days and a relationship that is cherished.

This person is also the same that must give you that "tough love" when you need a reality check. There are times in your college journey where you might struggle, fail a class, or feel like you won't be able to make it. You might find yourself swaying from your classes and getting off track. This person can help you refocus as well, remind you of your "why" when you need it the most and empower you to finish.

Generational Mentor

The generational mentor is an unconventional mentor that helps you understand current trends, cultural relevance, and a connection to the future. This mentorship helps you get an insight on the next generation of leaders and as you begin to think about life after college. Staying relevant is something that becomes more difficult as you get older and having someone in your circle that helps you with that is invaluable.

This can also help you while you are in college as well. When you think about your research, presentations, and delivery, staying relevant helps you deliver that message. "It is not what you say, but how you say it" is a popular and important saying. If you look to empower or enter a field that requires you to work with the next generation of leaders, finding a generational mentor is essential to stay ready.

Sponsorship

As you find yourself looking for mentors in different areas, also think about finding individuals, organizations, or even departments on campus that can sponsor you. Sponsorship is the act of someone/ something financially supporting or providing recommendations that can lead to financial gain. The idea of sponsorship is so important because money is a barrier for a lot of Latinx students—and there are so many ways to navigate around these issues.

Professional conferences, speaking engagements, service/ religious trips, etc. all costs a significant amount of money for the regular college student to attend. These opportunities in college can tremendously enhance your experience and build lifelong networks that will help you as a college student, but also beyond. Sponsors will fund these experiences for you with very few strings attached.

Sponsorship does not only equal funding. The other important aspect of sponsorship is how people talk about you in a room full of opportunities. You need people that will vouch for you when that scholarship, internship/ job opportunity, or grant money comes up. Having sponsors that will share, comment, and recommend you on social media is also a big plus.

During my undergraduate career, I received so many opportunities because other administrators, faculty, and departments sponsored me. I was able to travel to conferences, land jobs, explore internships, do community service projects in different states, and much more. I would never have had these experiences if it wasn't for the countless sponsors that paid for me.

Student Government Associations, clubs/ organizations, academic departments that fund student success, student leadership development offices are just some examples of departments on campus that can help sponsor you as a student. Administrators that hire students and sit on several institution committees can also be excellent sponsors. This is also another great reason why developing strong relationships with staff and faculty in your undergraduate career can pay dividends.

This is about accountability and making sure you succeed in your endeavors. Take the time to list your five mentors and one sponsor that you have established below. Remember what I said, connect with your mentor beforehand and make it official before listing them on the next page.

Academic Mentor_____

Career Mentor_____

Personal Mentor_____

Cultural Mentor_____

Generational Mentor _____

Sponsor _____

7
Pa'lante, Siempre, Pa'lante

This saying is in my office. Unfortunately, where I work, not too many people understand or know what it means. To the students that do know, it is a reminder to keep on pushing. To keep moving forward and being better than the day you were before. The saying may be short, but definitely powerful. In this chapter, we will talk about resiliency and the need to strengthen it during tough times.

Somos Poderosos

During your undergraduate career, you might find yourself at a low point of resilience—and maybe even feel like giving up. We have all been there. During these tough times, I do a lot of reflecting. I thought a lot about what my ancestors must have been through before me. The invasion of the land. The rape, slavery, captivity, and almost entire elimination of the indigenous culture. Most recent, my great grandparents, grandparents, and young mom fled to the United States for political asylum and left behind their entire lives in pursuit of a better future. This always helped me put my own trials and tribulations into perspective. Not to minimize or trivialize my own experience, but to show that we shall overcome.

Think about your own experience. You probably endured a ton of challenges in your childhood and upbringing. You might have had to face issues with divorce, death, socioeconomic challenges, mental health, etc., yet you still persevered.

Next time you might be having a hard day at school, reflect on all that you have accomplished. Every single bad day in your life, you have been able to survive it. You will survive and conquer your goals in college as well.

This certainty comes with a lot of pressure. You might be the only person in your family to go to college or your family might be counting on you to get a degree so you can help contribute. Whatever your circumstance might be, the pressure for you to succeed is very real.

Locus of Control

For the readers that have studied psychology, this part may be very familiar to you. Locus of Control is broken into two different parts, the inner and the outer locus of control. The inner locus of control focuses on the individual attributing their successes and failures to things that they have done. Outer locus of control focuses on the individual attributing their successes and failures to external factors. To strengthen resilience, people often challenge individuals to focus on developing their inner locus of control.

One way to do this is to ask yourself, "Do I have immediate control over this?" and if the answer is, "no"—then it might be time to shift your focus onto something else. By doing this, you are using your energy wisely and acting on aspects of your life that you can improve right now.

Let's utilize an example. There is a professor that is completely difficult to work with. You can say that the professor is out to get you. You can even say that the professor is going to actively fail you. In this situation, you will need to focus on the area you have most control over. Submitting quality assignments on time, meeting with the professor during office hours to discuss areas of improvement, sitting in the front of the class or cutting down on distractions, participation during lectures, etc. By focusing on those areas, you will give yourself a better chance at passing the class than focusing on the professor and their actions.

This is not to say that one locus of control is better than another. Understanding that certain aspects of your life are outside of your control is healthy. There are issues we face every day that are systemic and affect our lives in direct ways. However, this is a lesson on resilience and resilience is built by changing perspective and overcoming challenges, no matter how small or large they might be.

You Failed A Class—Now What?

Despite doing your very best, there could be a time in your academic career that you might fail a class. This can be a gut-wrenching failing for most students. You might feel like you are not capable or that it might be time to change your major. There are a couple of different things you can do to bounce back after failing a class.

Register for the class the next semester. You know what to expect now that you have taken the class and hopefully you can reflect on where you went wrong the first time. The definition of insanity is doing the same thing over and over again expecting different results, so hopefully, you learn from the failure and make changes. Also, at most institutions, when you retake the course and pass it, the previous grade is wiped away. Check with your individual institution's academic policy first.

Take the class with a different professor. Perhaps, the professor you took the first time has a teaching style that is not suitable to your needs. If that is the case, try to find another professor that teaches the same course. Consult with your academic advisor and other students in the major to gain some additional insight on other professors.

Take the class at another institution. This one is a little bit tricky because you will need to gain permission from your current institution first. Once you do, you can register to take the class at a community college or another 4-year institution. This can sometimes be cheaper and give you an opportunity to take it with a better professor that is suitable to your learning style.

Reevaluate and reflect. This is a major key. Why did you fail the course? Is it a major requirement or an elective? Taking the course over again might be the most logical choice, but sometimes, it is better to move on after taking the L. It is important to look introspectively and ask yourself some hard hitting questions. Is this the right major for you? Are you doing this because you want to or because you are facing the pressure from your family? These are important things to consider as you look to turn this L into a Lesson.

Embracing Failures

Failure is truly life's best teacher. When I look back at all the times I failed at something, I either have a funny story to tell or a valuable lesson to share. I am going to share with you one of my most valuable failures. I thought I wanted to be a teacher. As a first gen student, I wasn't too aware of career options and I locked myself into education from the start. I wanted to go back to my local high school, teach and inspire students from my hometown while giving back to the community.

I studied education for 4 years as my major until my 5th and final year *(yes I did 5 years in undergrad. Ain't no shame in my game)* when I had to take the Praxis.[12] I was already a questionable test taker and the Praxis was the hardest test I have ever had to take in my life. I took the test 3 times. The first time I failed it by 5 points. The second time by 3 points. The third time by 1 point.

I was broke after paying for the test three times, exhausted from studying, and stressed because I did not know what to do with my life after college. I had a plan and the one test was keeping me from fulfilling my goals. I sat with my mentors and explained to them how I was feeling. I learned through some hard conversations that I loved education, but not in the way I envisioned it when I entered college. Failing those Praxis exams time and time again pushed me to find a different way to be an educator. Embracing those failures pushed me to apply for and finish my graduate degree in education. Currently, I work as an administrator at a college, teaching in a much different way than I ever thought I would.

This is my long way to say—embrace your failures. When you are winning, everything is good. Winning can keep you complacent and allow you to not work on your weaknesses. Failure gives us room to look at our weaknesses and do something differently.

---

[12] Praxis: State exam in NJ that requires a certain score to pass and become teacher certified.

It is time to change the narrative on fearing failure. Failure is an opportunity to develop and be better than before and we should not fear that.

To conclude this chapter, feel free to fill in the image on the next page. Think about a current challenge you are facing in school, work, or in life. When you are at a low point, think about this image and fill in the areas that you have control over and what you do not have control over. This will help you reframe your thinking and focus your efforts on actionable items you can implement.

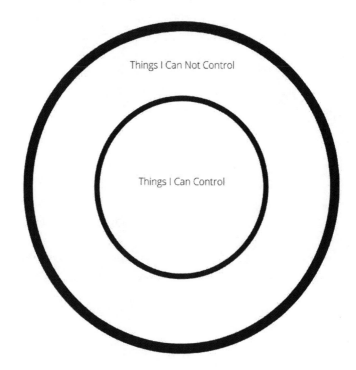

Things I Can Not Control

Things I Can Control

8
Social Media Education

Social media has changed the way we interact forever. The ability to instantly connect with others or put your ideas/ thoughts into the world is something that can directly influence your education. For those of us that have smart phones, we have super computers at the palm of our hands that can search information in a matter of seconds. This chapter will discuss how to utilize the power of social media to boost your educational experiences.

Connect with Groups on Facebook

I know, I know—Facebook? Some of you might not even have an account anymore. However, Facebook groups have a wealth of knowledge and people that update the groups consistently. I have seen job postings, idea sharing, virtual project collaborations, and even webinars that have been hosted for FREE.

The group can be educational or can be something you are into as a hobby. Maybe you are looking to build on a skillset that you hope to make money with. Facebook groups can help connect you with the information you need and put you on the right track. Instead of mindlessly scrolling at funny videos and sharing memes, you can utilize this to help you further your education.

This is certainly powerful for students that are at institutions that lack resources. For example, if you are interested in marine biology and that is not offered at your institution, connecting with Facebook groups can provide you with internship opportunities, job postings, volunteers for events, etc. This can help supplement the lack of tangible experience you might not be getting at your current institution.

Insta-Stalk Institutions

This was one of my favorite things to do as an undergrad student. I know, I am weird. I would take time to look at what other institutions are doing and posting about on their social media accounts. This goes out to any of my student leaders, event coordinators, or even Resident Assistants. Looking at what other institutions are doing can be an easy way to find some cool ideas to steal and tweak to make it fit at your institution. The best ideas are stolen!

Some institutions even offer free courses or free programs through their social media accounts. If your institution struggles with online programs, take advantage of what some of these other schools are offering. Having some friends at other institutions also makes this easier to take advantage of what other programs offer.

Find Digital Professors

You might be learning a lot of things at your institution, but are they around subject areas that you really want to learn about? Finding digital professors can help round out your educational experience or give you the opportunity to learn a new skill/ trade. There is a digital professor on social media for every field imaginable. You want to learn how to play video games? Learn how to make some delicious snacks? Learn how to manage your finances? There is a digital professor out there for you!

You can also find a digital professor that can help you enhance your academic experience within your major. If you are an upperclassmen and have a unique research focus that is not offered at your institution, find professors that have similar interests as you on social media. You can gain valuable experience from them and even reach out to schedule a time to chat; the worst thing they can say is no!

¿Dónde Está Mi Gente?

For students that attend PWIs - this one is for you. It can be very lonely and difficult as a Latinx student. Some institutions have less than 100 Latinx students on the entire campus! This can make it extra difficult to feel at home and have some sense of belonging. By utilizing social media, you can connect with local, culturally based organizations and meet others that remind you of home.

You can also be strategic and connect with other student leaders across local colleges. This is especially powerful when you want to learn about what other students are going through that share a similar identity as you. You can share common struggles and best practices with each other. Developing a strong group like this across different campuses can help bring issues to the forefront and force institutions to change. You can also utilize a group like this to put on larger cultural events to educate the community and also to learn more about your own people.

9
Student Organizations

Supplementing Your Academic Experience

Your academic experience is a huge part of your college experience, but not your entire experience. There are a variety of things you can do to supplement that experience and being involved with your institution's student government organization can be that experience you need to supplement your experience. The experiences you have here can help you in interviews, applications, and to build your resume. In this chapter, we will talk about the various benefits you can receive by being involved in your student government organization.

Running a Club/ Managing others

One of the most tangible experiences you can receive is personnel management. Companies and employers want to know how you operate while working with others. Being able to manage your executive board as a President or holding a position that requires someone to report to you is great experience you can use to sell yourself in interviews. Running a club is almost like running a non-profit organization. You will be asked to do events that benefit the community and manage a budget. You have to write reports to receive funding and prove you are an organization that contributes to the community. Even if you do not want to run a non-profit organization, the skills here are transferable to most professional settings.

Financial Management

Managing a club requires strong financial management. Most clubs will have some type of budget allocated to them. Regardless of the budget size, learning how to manage the funds and appropriately utilize them throughout the course of the semester or academic year is a major skill to have. You will need to learn how to be resourceful with the funds allocated to you.

Depending on your budget and club, it might be fiscally responsible to work collaboratively with other clubs. This level of partnership can help you develop good business practices and enhance your ability to work with others. You would have to think about how much funds you want to offer, how the profits will be shared, and who will be responsible for managing that process before/ after the event.

Your ability to manage finances will be tested and this is a great, low-stakes way to help build some strong skills. As you go on to manage your own non-profits and budgets in your own careers, you can draw on some of the tangible experiences you had running your club.

Culturally Based Organizations

Most institutions will offer a variety of culturally based organizations on campus. They can be social clubs under the Student Government Organization, affinity clubs[13] under different departments, or Greek Letter Organizations *(we will get into this in the next chapter)*. Culturally based organizations can be very appealing to students that are seeking out others that have shared lived experiences or are actively seeking to learn more about other cultures.

By involving yourself in a culturally based organization, you can quickly build experiences with others from diverse backgrounds. I immediately went and found my culturally based organizations on campus because I value connecting with others that look like me. I felt safe in that space and was able to build strong relationships with those that attended. You might even find some folks that can help you in other areas on campus as well!

Academic Clubs

Involving yourself with an academic club is another way to compliment your educational experience. Are you looking for a writer's group, research group, or study group?

---

[13] Affinity Club: A forum or group of people that share a similar identity, experience, or ideology.

Find your academic clubs on campus that are tied to specific majors. These clubs can help you increase your contact to the smartest students in your major. You can pick up some valuable gems from them that can help your academic journey be a little bit easier. Academic clubs also have programming requirements as well. You can potentially connect with other faculty members in the department. Through the programming efforts, you may find yourself earning extra credit for participating or simply just grasping the material at a much faster rate.

Personally, I learn much more quickly by doing something than by sitting in a lecture. I found that by involving myself in academic clubs, I was able to find ways to apply the things I learned in the classroom into projects, programs, and valuable discussions outside the classroom. I did not feel like I was doing "extra" work by being part of an academic club and I felt like the work in the club helped me master the material.

Building Relationships

The most impactful part of being involved in these different areas is the ability to build relationships. Developing strong relationships is a huge part of being successful at your institutions. Developing and strengthening relationships has proven to boost students' ability to succeed and graduate at their institutions. Therefore, the more connected you become, the more likely you will be to finish.

Building relationships within your clubs and organizations on campus instantly connects you to the most influential people on your campus. Students that are involved have been proven to have higher GPAs, significantly higher rates of graduation, and higher rates of graduating with full-time employment.

Think about it—the folks you are spending your time with now in clubs and organizations are usually people with high work ethic. They have ambitions to be great at whatever they do and are very connected people. Building relationships with folks like these can help set you up with valuable networks for when you leave college. These are the same folks that might run for public office, start businesses, and be leaders in their own fields within a couple of short years. Cultivate those relationships.

10
Fraternity & Sorority Life

Fraternities[14] and Sororities[15] also known as Greek Letter Organizations (GLOs) although are considered student organizations, they are slightly different than the types of clubs I mentioned previously. Fraternities and Sororities have a rich culture, with some organizations dating back to the last century. Some predominately black and white organizations have surpassed the century mark! I will briefly touch on a few different types of GLOs for you to explore. In this chapter, we will explore the benefits of fraternities and sororities and commonly asked questions about Greek Letter Organizations.

Types of Organizations

To a person from the outside looking in, the three letters are all the same. However, there are different types of organizations for you to consider. Personally, I am in a GLO myself and have enjoyed all the experiences I have been able to gain from it. There has been a ton of professional development opportunities, brotherhood, and areas that I have been able to make an impact on.

---

[14] Fraternity: A group of people brought together because of common interest. Generally, this is a group of men, but also refers to co-ed organizations and many sororities are officially fraternities.
[15] Sorority: A GLO for women. This term was developed after Fraternity and adopted by women organizations

This chapter will give you some of my own personal experiences with my own knowledge of the fraternity and sorority world.

If you are considering joining a GLO, it is extremely important that you take your time to make this decision. This will be an organization that you will be a part of for the rest of your life and there is a financial component to be active, doubling the need to think your decision through wisely. I would strongly recommend you get on Google and do your independent research on any organization you might be interested in. Check your website, social media pages, and other news that might be connected to that specific organization before committing your time and money!

Nationals & Locals: I wanted to begin by stating the difference between national and local GLOs. National organizations have a national headquarters and have chapters located around the country. Local GLOs are generally only located on that specific institution or have very few chapters in the immediate region. There are pros and cons to both and it depends solely on what the individual is looking for and hoping to gain from their experience.

Predominately White Organizations: These are GLOs that have an overwhelmingly majority of white people. Most of these organizations have been around for a very long time and are also large in numbers.

Culturally Based Organizations: These are GLOs that have been founded by a diverse group of people. Most culturally based organizations have specific identities they cater to, but are not exclusive to (i.e. African American, Latinx, Southeast Asian, Chinese, etc.)

Co-Ed Service Organizations: Most GLOs have community service as a pillar or tenant within their organization. Co-Ed Service GLOs are strictly service based and if you are interested, offer the ability to be in another GLO.

New Member Process

Each organization will offer a new member education process for each person to complete. The new member process will teach new members the history and traditions of the organization. Most organizations have a process that will span for several weeks at a time. The purpose for these processes is to develop folks into productive new members and formulate strong bonds within the organization. New members will learn the secrets and traditions of the organization that has been passed down from generations.

Membership for Life

This is a key difference between being a part of a club and a GLO. Upon graduation, you will no longer serve as president of your club, but you will always be a member of your GLO. Even if you decide to be inactive[16] for a period of time, you will always have the opportunity to participate.

After graduation, you can continue to serve as an alumni advisor for undergraduate members, serve in leadership positions within different regions of the country or national leadership positions within your GLO. Alumni can work with other alumni to provide professional development opportunities or community service opportunities for undergraduate members to take advantage of.

I am very big on family and being in a GLO can mean having an extended family. If this is something that excites you—then being a part of a GLO can be for you!

---

[16] Inactive: A person that does not pay membership dues to their organization and is not involved.

Professional Development

Being involved means that you will always have opportunities to increase your professional development. GLOs offer a variety of different training for individuals to take advantage of. Some members may have specific skills in different trades that they offer to other members for a discount. Some organizations offer a variety of leadership positions that you can hold to enhance your professional development (i.e. national treasurer, community service chair, diversity and inclusion chair, etc.) The skills that you will obtain can be transferable to your career or can help you gain experience to land you the career you want.

Community Service

Community service is a huge part of being a part of a GLO. You can work with other members to develop strategic community service initiatives within your community, institution, or region at large. Being involved in a GLO means you already have a network to choose from and can find a group of members that are equally invested in a similar passion area.

One of my favorite community service initiatives was facilitating a high school conference for local high schools to learn more about college life. We started small at New Jersey City University with only my old high school in attendance (Union City High School).

The following year, we managed to have two and the next, four high schools with over 200 students in attendance. With the help of my organization alongside other GLOs, we were able to offer a onetime scholarship to one of the participants and give out invaluable information about college life.

Commonly Asked Questions About Greek Life

I will not be able to answer every question about Greek Life, but I will answer a handful of the top questions I have been asked regarding Greek Life.

Do they haze?

Each GLO will have an anti-hazing policy within their organization. Hazing is also illegal in many states and there are anti-hazing laws that need to be followed. Most institutions have a professional staff member that will be responsible to train students on these policies and most institutions have also developed their own anti-hazing policies. I would strongly recommend you ask all organizations what their stances are on hazing and to do as much research as possible.

Is Greek Life a cult?

Greek Life certainly has a ton of terminology and has its own culture, but it is definitely not a cult. There is a belief that certain GLOs idolize people or other random things. This could not be further from the truth. The organizations have strong history and traditions that people must learn to be a part of the organization, but they do not operate as cults nor are they religious in any way.

Is it true that you cannot talk to anyone while going through a new member process?

This is hard to comment on as so many organizations have different processes. Across the board, the new member process should be designed for new members to focus on learning the history of the organization and their traditions. The new member process should also help folks eliminate distractions. There has been a history of organizations participating in "social probation", in which the new member should be socializing with professors, administrators, immediate family, work colleagues, classmates, and other members in the organization. Sometimes, it might feel that way because the process is so time consuming, alongside your other day to day responsibilities.

Is Greek Life really like the movies?

I feel like the movies depict the worst or most extreme areas that Greek Life have to offer. I will be lying to you if I said there are no house parties or alcohol. You will certainly have the opportunity to be social and party, but that is a fraction of what Greek Life is about. Just like anything in life, the truth is often hidden between the extremes.

11
Disfrute el Colegio

All work and no play can make you a very dull person. Research has shown us that always focusing on work can lead to additional stress, burnout, and additional physical health risks. If no one has told you yet, it is okay to stop and have some fun! For me, it was difficult to not just find time, but find money to do things as well. This chapter will explore ways to have fun on a budget during your undergraduate career.

Sponsored Events & Trips

Most institutions will have programming that is offered to students throughout the semester. Most of the events offered will be free or dramatically subsidized for students. Look at the programming calendar and take advantage of your down time. Plan for these events in advance and think of them as a reward for all your hard work. Some events will be offered on campus or off-campus with transportation being covered. Giving yourself something to look forward to during the semester is a smart tactic to motivate yourself when school begins to get harder and harder.

Some institutions will even sponsor trips for select students to take advantage of. They could be weekend long to week long trips. These sponsored events can be conferences, leadership development retreats, or even service orientated trips. Institutions will sometimes cover the trip partially or even fully for students. Check in with the Student Life office and your email regularly for updates so you do not miss an amazing opportunity!

Study Abroad

I know, I know—study abroad? Con que dinero? I know study abroad can be challenging for students that struggle financially, but if this is something you always dreamed of doing—DO IT! Meet with your Study Abroad office and see what opportunities they are offering students. Some institutions will help you financially by covering your plane ticket or other expenses. You might learn about a scholarship that you can apply to that can help cover the costs. Personally, I never even tried to study abroad because of the financial implications and doubt I put in my own head. Before you begin to do that, meet with the staff and see what your options are at least. You never know.

Studying abroad is also not a long term commitment. You can study for an entire 16-week semester or you can do some smaller experiences. Most institutions are becoming more creative with their study abroad experiences and are offering shorter trips. They can be during your winter or spring break, or take place strategically for 2 to 3 weeks at a time. Since they are a shorter time commitment, they are more affordable and more reasonable for the average student.

Ideas for Spring/ Winter/ Summer Breaks

Depending on your circumstance, you might be able to maximize on the down time the academic year brings. There are built in breaks that last for a couple of days to a couple of months. I have decided to make a small list of budget ideas you can steal for your college breaks!

- *Staycation*
- *Trilogy Movie Night*
- *Spring Cleaning*
- *Go (Thrift) Shopping*
- *DIY Craft Project*
- *Visit Family*
- *Have A Cookout*
- *Road Trip*
- *Game Night*
- *Night out at the Museum*
- *Visit a National Park*
- *Check out local tourist attractions*

- *Learn a new skill online*
- *Binge a TV Series*
- *Start a bookclub with friends*
- *Volunteer somewhere you are passionate about*
- *Complete a puzzle*
- *Local comedy/ artist shows*
- *Host a Karaoke Night*
- *Hiking/ Camping/ Nature trip*

12
Con Qué Tiempo?

College is A LOT. If you have read up to this point, most of you may be wondering, "How can I manage all of this?" There is so much to do and so many extra things to take advantage of that it might feel like there's not enough time in the world to accomplish everything. In this chapter, we will explore different ways to stretch your time and some other strategies and tips to help you along the way.

El Trabajo y Las Estudias

For many of us, working throughout your undergrad career is a very real possibility. Some of you might need to work 15 to 20 hours while others might have to work full-time. Some of us have to help with bills or by sending money back home to our families. This can make getting your degree while also trying to take advantage of any extracurriculars a challenge.

It is important to ask yourself, what do you prioritize more? Your school or your job? By understanding this, you can begin to set some boundaries and expectations. If you value your job more, it is okay to go part-time and take less classes. If you value your schooling, speak with your employer about having a set schedule, limiting hours, and working around your school schedule.

Build your experience around your needs. Your needs will change from time to time depending on life events. Therefore, it is always good to reevaluate periodically. One semester, you might need to take all night classes while other semesters, you might need to take them during the day. Take into consideration time to commute from work to school and personal time (i.e. sleeping and eating!).

Work during the off times in the semester. If you work a job that can make you a lot of money during the summer and winter breaks, rack up more hours during those periods. Do your calculations of what you need before each semester begins. Hit your target goal during the break times so you can solely focus on academics and other activities during the semester. This works really well for folks that need separation between school and work, but still need to make money.

Find an institution and job that values both. Some institutions have a more traditional student population that majority of students do not have outside jobs. This will affect you because the institution will assume school is your #1 responsibility. The class schedules, parking situation, and finding advisors that can relate could be a major challenge.

Also, finding a job that values your education is important. Some employers might not care that you are pursuing your degree and will give you extra shifts during peak exam times. Find a job that will be flexible enough for you during the times you are in semester. Some jobs might even offer scholarships or tuition remission as part of the benefit package. If you find yourself at odds with your school or your job, it might be time to make a shift.

Finding a Balance

The key to learning how to manage it all is to work on finding a balance. You know yourself best. Sit down and reflect on your needs and ask yourself, when are you most productive? Do you need to have some fun before you work or do you need to work before you have fun? Building in breaks to spend time with family, doing something fun, or simply relaxing time is important to get through this college journey. This experience is a journey and not just a destination!

Know when you are at high stress times. Look ahead at your syllabi and plan ahead for those high stress times. You may have one week that has 4 major assignments due. Mark that week in your calendar at the beginning of the semester. See if you can flex some time off for your job during that week or try to get ahead on those assignments. Being able to plan ahead will help you do the work bit by bit, instead of staying up all night writing that paper before it is due.

Schedule fun in between. We will talk about this more in the next chapter, but make sure to have fun! Undergrad is a special time in your life and should be the time to have some fun as well. Build in break times in between to go hang with your friends in the cafeteria. Schedule a road trip with some friends. Take advantage of some cool events your institution hosts to hang with friends or make new friends. Have some fun in the midst of all that chaos!

Respecting Your Time

Put some respect on your time because it is invaluable. Something I like to share with the students I meet with is this: Time is the most valuable thing I can offer you, because once I spent it, it was gone. I cannot deposit it in my checking/ savings account. If I choose to spend my time with you, it is because I am INVESTING you in. Make some good investments with your time and watch it come back to you tenfold.

There are 168 hours in a week. Factor in the time you need to sleep (and make sure you do sleep!) and now you are looking at less than that. Develop a schedule that breaks down your day hour by hour. Plan the time you are going to eat, be in class, study, and down time. There are a ton of grid schedule templates online for you to utilize and fill in with your schedule.

Set reminders on your phone. Even if you are more of a planner person, setting reminders on your phone can help you when you get caught chatting with your friend in the student union building. The buzzing or ringing can keep you on schedule and on task when those random moments come up. I lived by my smartphone calendar application when I was in undergrad because it served almost as an electronic personal assistant.

Two for One

This is something I did throughout my entire undergrad career and it helped save me so much time. I purposely found ways to accomplish two things at the same time to maximize my experience and time. My first year, I changed part time jobs to something that allowed me to be more stationary (hotel front desk clerk). This helped me because during down times, I can do homework and get some studying in. During the overnight shifts, I was able to do larger scale assignments and even get out ahead in my class readings. If possible, find a job that offers this level of flexibility. Most jobs that are on campus will offer you more flexibility because they know you are a student first.

Look at different ways you can do this in your academic discipline. I was able to get academic credit and a paid internship in one. This put extra money in my pocket for an academic requirement I already needed. Consult with your academic advisor and your department to learn about different opportunities that they have offered in the past to students.

Find opportunities for leadership development that also offer some kind of financial benefit. Becoming more involved in your institution is something that has been mentioned in this book before, so might as well benefit from it other than experience. Some leadership opportunities might offer stipends, academic credit, meal plan/ housing credit, or even tuition reimbursement. Put some respect on your time and start asking what benefits come with your on campus leadership positions.

This is a little study hack that I utilized to get more time out of my day. Instead of listening to music, I would turn on my podcasts or my audiobooks for class. Whenever I had to commute or go on a long walk, I was able to do a little bit of homework on the way. I always carried my phone with me and even have written a couple of papers on my phone. Turning any "dead" time into productivity will help you in the long run. It will take some time to master the art of accomplishing two things at one time, but it is worth it!

Mix Methods Approach

The goal should be to find strategies that work for you to maximize your time. Some of the strategies I have suggested might not work for you. Perhaps, you will need a combination of different strategies. Whatever that maybe, it will most likely be a mix methods approach. There is no one size fits all model for managing time. The key is to continue to push yourself to try new ways to maximize your time. Try something for a while and see how it works for you before giving up on it.

There is a belief that if you do something for 21 days straight, it becomes a habit. Good or bad. Implement some of the time saving strategies listed above or try some of your own that you learned from someone else. On the bottom of this page, write down the 5 new strategies you will implement into your daily lives and write down the date you began. Reflect and revisit the strategies in a couple of weeks depending on what works for you.

1. _____

2. _____

3. _____

4. _____

5. _____

13
<u>Mental Health in the Latinx Community</u>

My own personal experiences make writing this chapter a difficult one, but I know it is an absolutely necessary topic for me to dive in on. Personally, I was raised in a very conservative Latinx household that did not believe in men being able to cry or express their emotions. Mental health was not spoken about in my household at all and not something I learned about until halfway through my undergraduate degree. Speaking from experience, I know how challenging it can be to talk about mental health to family members. Although there is more awareness promoted about mental health now than even 5 years ago, it is still very much taboo within the community. This chapter will dive into important mental health tenets to remember, how to take care of your mental health throughout college, and a ton of tips to take with you for beyond.

Unlearning Trauma Responses

Unlearning the trauma, you endured in your life is absolutely necessary to build stronger relationships in undergrad. Some of the trauma in our lives has forced us to develop some problematic responses. The inability to trust others and hyper independence is just the tip of the iceberg. I cannot tell you how many students I work with that are Latinx and have this massive barrier up.

It becomes difficult for them to connect with others on campus (even other students that look like them) and develop strong relationships. Some students are navigating issues of abandonment and self-love. The issues from our childhood will plague your future relationships if left unchecked.

To begin the unlearning process, it is necessary to reflect and check-in with yourself regularly. What are your triggers? How have you been feeling lately? As Bad Bunny said, *"Baby, la vida es un ciclo y lo que no sirve yo no lo reciclo."* It is time to work on leaving those problematic responses in the past and begin to formulate stronger bonds.

You Are More Than Your Titles

As a student, something I got caught up on a lot was titles. My titles were very important to me. They became a part of my identity. Whether it was being a RA, a friend, a high achieving student, a president, etc. When someone would ask me, "Tell me about yourself", I would find myself listing those same titles and jobs. You are more than your titles. You are more than your GPA, your major, and your productivity. In this social media generation, it is easy to find yourself scrolling, looking at everyone winning on your feed and find yourself not doing enough. Love yourself for who you are without comparing your timeline to anyone else's.

Imposter Syndrome

Imposter Syndrome is real, *mi gente*. It could happen during the application process, on orientation day, move-in day, or triggered throughout your undergraduate career. Imposter Syndrome is that internal dialogue in your head second guessing all your greatness. It can prevent you from being your best self and it is important to check-in with yourself routinely to keep it from letting those feelings manifest themselves in different ways.

I can tell you I have dealt with (and still to this very day) deal with imposter syndrome. I have felt multiple times that maybe I was just picked as a "diversity hire" so that an institution can look more inclusive. You might share similar feelings as I do right now. Recognize those feelings and deal with your emotions, but know that you are indeed powerful beyond measure. You are where you are for a reason and you have earned your spot. You are just as smart, talented, and driven as everyone else. Alright, let me get off my soap-box and give you some tangible pieces on dealing with this.

Reach out and ask for help. Whenever you are having these thoughts, communicate with those closest to you. Have some of your closest friends give you a pep talk. If they are written messages, keep them in your notes or a folder and read them over whenever you are feeling overwhelmed. Schedule a call to one of your mentors (another important reason to have them!) to vent, but also so they can remind you of your awesomeness. Your thoughts and the language you speak to yourself is powerful. Start by building good habits and being mindful of what you say to yourself every day. As the great Lauryn Hill has said, *"You can't win if you ain't right from within."*

On Campus Mental Health Services

Go ahead and check how much a local therapist is charging per hour to see a client. It's out of control right? Mental health is just as important as physical health, but the services are also staggering to folks that are already struggling to make ends meet. This is why it is important to take advantage of the mental health services your institution offers you already.

Most institutions have some form of Wellness/Counseling Center. You can see licensed psychologists, counselors, or therapists on a regular basis throughout the academic year. I strongly, strongly, STRONGLY encourage the use of these services. It helps to talk about the things that are affecting you in your life with a mental health professional and not only your friends. They have been trained to be great listeners and offer professional strategies on making positive strides in your daily lives.

If you were like me, I was very hesitant going in at first. I did not want to be seen by anyone walking into the office for fear of people stigmatizing me. After the first session, I certainly felt more at ease and I knew that what was said in the sessions would not be repeated to anyone. If you had a negative experience at first, try another mental health professional. Finding a mental health professional for you is all about fit and what you need at the moment.

Self-Care is Important

Self-care was something that was hard for me to develop. I was always moving so quickly day to day—always focused on the next project, assignment, meeting, or class. Self-care was hard for me because I felt like it was deterring me from accomplishing my goals. However, self-care helped me enjoy the moment. I tried many things as "self-care" before finding what stuck for me.

The goal is to find something that truly relaxes you. Not something that increases your productivity, because self-care is not about how much more productive you can be. Self-care is nuanced and personal. It is impossible to tell me what exactly it should be.

I want you to imagine a stamina bar over your head. Depending on what you are doing, the stamina bar drains throughout the day. Some things are harder for you than others, so the stamina bar can become depleted faster than you think. People often engage in self-care when their stamina bar is completely depleted. But, the trick is to engage in small self-care exercises BEFORE you become completely drained. Ask yourself, what reenergizes you? Is it a nap? A conversation with your mentor? A movie? Self-care does not have to be this giant spa day that most people think it is.

Are you still unsure of what your self-care practices are? Check out this curated list of tips to start!

- *Read more books*
- *Sleep 7 to 8 hours a day*
- *Keep track of positive compliments. Read them when you need them.*
- *Schedule a call with someone you look up to*
- *Schedule a day to disconnect with the world and connect with yourself*
- *Ask for that extension on a project or assignment*
- *Turn off email notifications on your phone*

- *Blast that salsa/ bachata/ merengue/ reggaeton/ cumbia and clean your physical space*
- *Pick a show. Pick a day. Binge watch a season or show*
- *Visit your nearest animal shelter and pet the puppies!*
- *Plan a staycation*
- *Dress for success. Wear your best fit on a day you need a little more swag*
- *Say 10 things out loud that you are proud of everyday*
- *Write a thank you email to someone close to you*
- *Say No. That's it. That's the tip.*
- *Find ways to eat healthier. Your body can't function on poor fuel.*
- *Make a photo album of your favorite photos*
- *Listen to a new podcast*
- *Learn a new life skill*
- *Start a journal. Write at least one sentence before going to bed each day.*
- *Get some physical exercise for 30 minutes a day*
- *Take a long drive*
- ***Your self-care is non-negotiable***

14
We Are Not a Monolith

I am going to say that most institutions, especially predominately white institutions, have no idea on how to properly support their Latinx student population. We are complex and nuanced people that no "one size fits all" model will work for. We span different generations, sexual, racial and socioeconomic identities. The institutions that we attend, hell, the world we live in today will make assumptions of our abilities, likes, dislikes because of the color of our skin, our accent, or the language we speak.

You Do Not Speak For All Latinx Folks…And Neither Do I

I want to share with you an exchange I had with a previous acquaintance I had in college. Let's call him *Fulano* [17] for the sake of the story. Fulano travelled to different countries for weeks at a time and one time he travelled to Cuba. After being in Cuba for two weeks, he slid into my DMs with 100% seriousness to ask me,

"Hey bro, are you sure you are really Cuban? Cause you darker skin and I don't see any dark skin Cubans here."

---

[17] Fulano/a: A Latinx term in Spanish for a completely random person.

And instead of *mándanlo para el carajo* like I should have, I decided to tell him a little about himself. I informed him that Google is free—and instead of asking me to do additional labor, that he could have just used the internet to answer his ridiculous question.

And folks, that is just one of the many examples of what some people will do. They will meet you and assume everyone with your background is the same. They will claim to be "diverse" because they have "a friend" from a specific background, identity, socioeconomic status, or religious affiliation and suddenly believe they are content experts on your culture and background.

As annoying as dealing with fulanos in personal relationships may be, this is increasingly problematic with fulanos that are in power. They will meet with you once and claim they know how to work with all Latinx students moving forward. Some of the language they might use and even policies implemented are problematic. When engaging with fulanos, please continue to remind them that their personal experience with you does not equal professional/ cultural experience across the board. Challenge them to do their own work. They need to continually do the work and check their biases at the door because they hold the power over other folks that look like us.

Language Does Not Make You Less Latinx

Unfortunately, there is so much prejudice within our own people. Folks that do not know the Spanish language often are looked as "less than" by other Latinx. It is so unfortunate when our own people ostracize each other instead of building each other up. There are so many reasons as to why Latinx people did not have the privilege of learning the Spanish language.

If you are one of those Latinx, please know that you are still a part of the community and loved. If you know the language, please continue to spread that knowledge and culture with other Latinx. Let's focus on strengthening the community instead of dividing it. We all know that especially in today's climate, we have enough of that division.

Challenging the Status Quo

At our institutions, it is important to challenge that status quo. Push the administration at your institutions to do what is right by students, especially marginalized students, to feel safe. We all have some level of privilege that we can exercise to increase the quality of life for others. Whether that is a meeting, video, letter, or even a simple conversation with the administration, you have the ability to influence the folks in power. I hope they do not think that they can place you in a monolith you don't belong in.

Consejo De Amigo

As a Cuban & Dominican Latino male, I grew up listening to a lot of Spanish music at home. One of my favorite things to do to this day is wake up on a Saturday morning, blast my Bachata playlist, and go in a cleaning binge around the house. This chapter is titled *Consejo De Amigo*, and if you read this far into the book, I would like to consider you a friend. This chapter title is to pay homage to the greatest bachatero of all time—Anthony Santos and hit you with some of the best *consejos* I have received in my undergraduate career.

Maximize student discounts

This is something that has blown up in the last couple of years. More and more companies are offering student discounts for anyone that has a @edu email address. When you are purchasing anything new, taking your bank accounts or credit cards, or are going to any attraction, ask if they have a student discount! Be sure to have your school ID handy and save some coins. Some popular discounts are on Spotify or Apple music premium being 50% off with a student account. Also, you can install all the Microsoft Office programs for free on your personal devices!

Go to as many events in college as possible

Your tuition dollars do not only pay for your classes. They pay for the resources and activities your institution puts on. Attend as many of these events as you can, even if they may not interest you. Majority of the time, there will be FREE food as well—so plan accordingly!

Check your student email once a day

If you do not have your school email on your phone yet, Ima need you to put it on right now. Scroll down and check it like you would your Instagram feed. You will receive emails about events, food, scholarships, job opportunities, classes, etc. It is absolutely necessary for you to check that email at least once a day.

Get an on-campus job

You may already have a job off-campus, but I still recommend getting one even if it is for 5 to 10 hours a week. You can continue to boost your resume and build some valuable relationships with professional staff.

Oftentimes, they will be willing to help you secure another job on campus and can write you a strong recommendation letter for future employment. You can see if you are eligible for the Federal Work Study[18] program with your Financial Aid department or check departments on campus for openings.

Make friends with seniors in your major

You may meet some upperclassmen in student clubs/organizations or even at an event your academic department may hold. You can learn about their experience going through the program. This can help you secure the go-to professors to take, key lecture notes for class, and important major specific information you should know.

Get involved on campus

Join a club or two on campus. You can learn a lot about an area you have always been interested in and gain more experience. There are cultural, academic, and social clubs at almost every institution. Getting involved is a great resume booster and an easy way to build stronger relationships. We will take a deep dive in a later chapter.

---

[18] Federal Work Study: A program that grants a student with financial need a select amount of funds per semester to work in any department on campus. Usually between 5 to 10 hours a week.

Meet with your academic advisor. Early and often

I cannot begin to tell you how many people I have met that needed to do an extra semester because they were not properly advised academically. Yes, you can easily elect to do your academic scheduling on your own, but remember what I said about utilizing your resources? Your academic program might change during the course of your time at the institution or your academic advisor can find a way for one course to count for two requirements. Always review your academic plan with your advisor on a semester basis.

Schedule "down" time for yourself

College can feel like you are on go, go, go 24/7/365, but it is vital to build in routine breaks. Your college career is a journey and taking care of yourself throughout is needed to avoid burnout. Think of scheduling something for yourself on a consistent basis (weekly, monthly, and yearly) to give you something good to look forward to.

Have a calendar—and use it!

Utilize a Google calendar or even your school email's calendar function. Schedule in all your classes, events, job responsibilities, studying times, meetings, and even personal appointments. This is something I was so adamant about in my undergrad. I had my entire life schedule on my smartphone calendar and the reminders served as my personal assistant to keep me from losing track of my life.

Do Not Buy Your Books Before The Semester Begins

This one might sound confusing, but seriously, wait until you take your first class with the professor before buying the book. Sometimes, professors will not even utilize the book and you just spent hundreds of dollars for no reason. Some professors will even give you work around (i.e. the book can be loaned to you by the library and you can take pictures of the pages or scan copies). Other times, you can work with a friend in the class to go half on the book and save you some money.

Those are some quick college related consejos from an older veteran to you. Take them or leave them, but I hope if you are this far in the book, you take them with love. Speaking of love, I wanted to leave you with some of my own personal favorite Latinx sayings on the next page. I hope they bring you memories of your family or you get to pass them on to your friends.

Sana, Sana, Culito De Rana, Si no Sanas Hoy, Sanas Mañana

El Pueblo Unido, Jamás Será Vencido

Ojos que no ven, corazón que no siente

Nunca es tarde si la dicha es buena

El que lee mucho y anda mucho, ve mucho y sabe mucho

El que no llora, no mama.

Dime con quién andas y te diré quién eres

Al que madruga Dios lo ayudo

Te conozco, bacalao, aunque vengas disfrazao

Mas sabe el diablo por viejo que por diablo

Conclusion

If you have read this far, THANK YOU. I appreciate you for being a part of this journey with me. I hope that throughout the chapters, you have been able to find little nuggets to take with you to increase your overall development at your institution. The goal was always to share my knowledge with as many students—particularly Latinx students—by combining my own lived experiences. I have had a pleasure writing this book and will certainly continue to work on another one!

Success is difficult to measure. Some folks might find success in finishing a degree in four years while others might find success in completing it debt free. However you define success, the purpose of the book was to offer multiple strategies to maximize the time you have at your institutions. You all pay so much money to be at college. You should be getting every single pennies worth from your experience. I am sure that this book will put you steps closer to your goals.

Please share these *consejos* with your friends. Continue focusing on building your tribes and taking care of yourself. Challenge the institutions to reflect and provide better and more equitable opportunities for Latinx students. Find those dope people on your campus that will ride with you and hold them close. You deserve all of that and more. Now it is time to stop blocking your blessings and do the work!

About The Author

Alvert is a Latino male from Union City, New Jersey. Inspired by other educators in an urban environment, Alvert knew he wanted to serve his community and work with students one day. Alvert is a well-rounded professional in Student Affairs with extensive experience in Residence Life, Fraternity & Sorority Life, Academic Advising, and Opportunity Programs for First Generation College students. He is a dynamic speaker that focuses on building a relationship with his audience and tying theory with practicality. During his undergraduate career, Alvert held a variety of student leadership roles including being a two-term student body president.

Alvert has a Masters in Higher Education Administration & Leadership from Montclair State University. As a Trill or Not Trill member, Alvert works as a content curator and presents on leadership, group dynamics, and diversity/inclusion and equity topics. His passion areas are working with first generation students of color and access programs. Alvert has presented at colleges and universities along the east coast and has presented at the largest student leadership conference in the country, the National Conference on Student Leadership (NCSL). Alvert also works with the educational institute, Trill or Not Trill as a content curator and speaker.

For More Information, visit

www.TheAlvertHernandez.com

Made in United States
Orlando, FL
17 January 2024